WITHDRAWN

LIGHTNING BOLT BOOKS™

Let's visit the Lake

Buffy Silverman

Lerner Publications ◆ Minneapolis

Lerner Publications Company
A division of Lerner Publishing Group, Inc.
241 First Avenue North
Minneapolis, MN 55401 USA

For reading levels and more information, look up this title at www.lernerbooks.com.

Library of Congress Cataloging-in-Publication Data

Names: Silverman, Buffy, author.
Title: Let's visit the lake / by Buffy Silverman.
Description: Minneapolis : Lerner Publications, [2017] | Series: Lightning bolt books. Biome explorers | Includes bibliographical references and index.
Identifiers: LCCN 2015050902 (print) | LCCN 2016011234 (ebook) | ISBN 9781512411935 (lb : alk. paper) | ISBN 9781512412314 (pb : alk. paper) | ISBN 9781512412017 (eb pdf)
Subjects: LCSH: Lakes—Juvenile literature. | Lake ecology—Juvenile literature.
Classification: LCC GB1603.8 .S55 2017 (print) | LCC GB1603.8 (ebook) | DDC 577.63—dc23

LC record available at http://lccn.loc.gov/2015050902

Manufactured in the United States of America
1-39695-21306-4/6/2016

Table of Contents

A Journey to the Lake

Imagine sitting by a lake on a summer evening. Frogs croak. Dragonflies dart. Herons catch fish near the lake's surface.

A lake biome is home to
many plants and animals.
Plants grow in shallow water.
Animals wade and swim.

Lakes are found on all seven of Earth's continents and on every kind of land—even in the tundra and the desert!

This map shows the Great Lakes. Together, these lakes make up the largest body of fresh water on Earth.

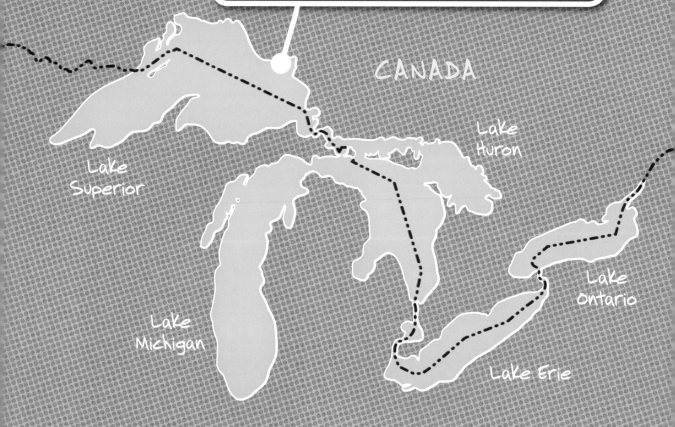

CANADA

Lake Superior

Lake Huron

Lake Michigan

Lake Ontario

Lake Erie

UNITED STATES

Lakes form in low areas in the land. Water flows from the land to the low spot. Gradually the lake fills.

Rain, snow, ice, streams, and groundwater fill a lake. Most lakes contain fresh water.

A pond is a small, shallow lake. Plants grow across this pond.

Some lakes are huge. Others are small. Lakes can be deep or shallow.

Animals in the Lake

A dragonfly nymph sits on the lake bottom. Its jaw shoots out and grabs a bug. The nymph squirts water from its tail. It streaks forward like a rocket.

Many insects lay eggs in lakes. Young insects live underwater. They breathe with gills. They climb out of the lake when it's time to become adults.

This mayfly rests on a leaf. Soon it will be ready to produce young.

Crayfish hide at the bottom of lakes and dig burrows under rocks. They feast on fish eggs, snails, insects, and plants. They use their sharp claws to keep predators away.

This crayfish hides among the leaves at the bottom of a lake.

Largemouth bass swim in clear water. They hide among plants and eat insects, crayfish, and smaller fish.

A bullfrog rests in warm, still water. It is hidden among floating plants. Its tongue zips out and grabs its prey.

Bullfrogs will eat whatever they can fit in their mouths—even other frogs.

This snake is called a northern water snake.

A water snake suns itself on a tree branch. It drops into the lake below. The snake herds a school of fish. It swallows one fish after another.

A loon glides across a lake.
It dives below the surface
and paddles with its powerful
feet. It chases small fish and
swallows them.

A family of beavers huddles in its lodge. The lodge has an underwater entrance. The beavers dive underwater to bring back sticks to the lodge.

Beavers eat bark and twigs.

Plants in the Lake

Green plants grow in and around a lake habitat. They grow in clear water where there is sunlight.

Green plants and algae need sunlight to make food.

Many plants grow on the surface of a lake. Tiny duckweed plants float in the water.

Masses of green algae also float on lakes. They look like slime. Algae release spores that grow into more algae.

This lake is covered in slimy, green algae.

Some plants grow below the surface. A bladderwort has small sacs on it. The sacs trap tiny water animals. The plant digests these animals.

Other plants grow both below and above the water. Pickerelweed grows near the shore. Green leaves and flowers reach up above the water. Long stems stretch to the muddy bottom.

Cattails also grow in shallow water. Their roots creep along the lake bottom. New stems shoot up from these roots.

23

Living in the Lake

Plants and animals depend on one another in a lake. Green plants and algae use energy from the sun to make food and release oxygen into the water.

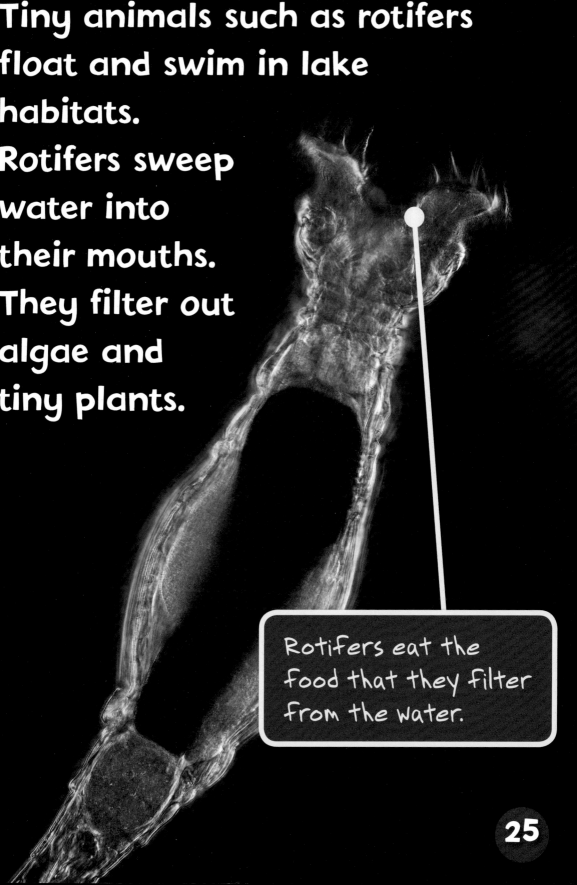

Tiny animals such as rotifers
float and swim in lake
habitats.
Rotifers sweep
water into
their mouths.
They filter out
algae and
tiny plants.

Rotifers eat the
food that they filter
from the water.

Insects, snails, and worms feast on rotifers and other floating food. Fish and frogs catch these small animals. Larger fish and birds eat smaller fish.

Over many years, the lake ecosystem begins to change. A lake starts to fill in and become land. Then other plants and animals can live there.

Wind and rain push dirt and leaves into the lake. They sink to the bottom.

Eventually, the lake fills up and becomes new land.

27

People and the Lake

Many people love to visit lakes. People enjoy fishing, boating, and swimming on lakes. But human activity can harm lakes. Chemicals from farms, lawns, and factories seep into lakes. These chemicals make algae grow too quickly. Then fish and other animals can't survive.

Everyone can help keep lakes clean and safe. We can use cleaning products that don't harm lakes. We can grow gardens and grass without adding harmful chemicals. We can plant trees that keep soil from washing into lakes.

Biome Extremes

- Deepest lake: Lake Baikal, Russia, 5,370 feet (1,637 meters)

- Largest lake: Caspian Sea, 760 miles (1,225 kilometers) long

- Largest lake fish: white sturgeon, 20 feet (6 m) long and 1,500 pounds (680 kilograms)

- World's smallest flowering plant: *Wolffia*, a type of duckweed growing in lakes. It would take five thousand *Wolffia* plants to fill a thimble!

- Highest lake for boats: Lake Titicaca in the Andes Mountains between Bolivia and Peru, 12,500 feet (3,810 m) above sea level

- Lowest lake: Dead Sea, between Israel and Jordan, 1,300 feet (395 m) below sea level

Glossary

algae: plantlike living creatures that make food and live in lakes

biome: a group of plants and animals in a large area, such as a desert or forest

ecosystem: an area of connected living and nonliving things

fresh water: water that is not salty

gills: organs that can take oxygen from water

groundwater: water that is underground

habitat: the natural home of plants or animals

lake: a body of water that is surrounded by land

nymph: a young insect that does not change completely as it grows

predator: an animal that lives by killing and eating other animals

prey: an animal that is hunted by another animal for food

Further Reading

Franco, Betsy. *Pond Circle.*
New York: Margaret K. McElderry Books,
2009.

Freshwater: Kids Do Ecology
http://kids.nceas.ucsb.edu/biomes/freshwater.html

Parker, Steve. *Eyewitness Pond and River.* New
York: DK, 2011.

Ponds: Young People's Trust for the Environment
https://ypte.org.uk/factsheets/ponds/what-is-a-pond

Ponds and Lakes: Missouri Botanical Garden
http://www.mbgnet.net/fresh/lakes/index.htm

Salas, Laura Purdie. *Water Can Be . . .* Minneapolis:
Millbrook Press, 2014.

Index

Photo Acknowledgments

The images in this book are used with the permission of: © Leena Robinson/Shutterstock.com, p. 2; © Jne Valokuvaus/Shutterstock.com, p. 4; © Neil Lockhart/Dreamstime.com, p. 5; © Laura Westlund/Independent Picture Service, pp. 6, 27; © iStockphoto.com/kekko73, p. 7; © Cheriecokeley/Dreamstime.com, p. 8; © iStockphoto.com/jkreslake, p. 9; © Vitalii Hulai/Shutterstock.com, p. 10; © asawinimages/Shutterstock.com, p. 11; © Matteo photos/Shutterstock.com, p. 12; © Beth Swanson/Shutterstock.com, p. 13; © Bruce Macqueen/Dreamstime.com, p. 14; © iStockphoto.com/rpbirdman, p. 15; © iStockphoto.com/Lynn_Bystrom, p. 16; © Donald M. Jones/Minden Pictures, p. 17; © Tomas1111/Dreamstime.com, p. 18; © Dawna Moore/Dreamstime.com, p. 19; © Nagel Photography/Shutterstock.com, p. 20; © blickwinkel/Hecker/Alamy, p. 21; © iStockphoto.com/gsermek, p. 22; © Skorpionik00/Shutterstock.com, p. 23; © walshphotos/Shutterstock.com, p. 24; © Frank Fox/Science Source, p. 25; © Kletr/Shutterstock.com, p. 26; © Elephantopia/Dreamstime.com, p. 31.

Front cover: © George Burba/Shutterstock.com.

Main body text set in Johann Light 30/36.